For Mum

This book is dedicated to you Mum, you have been there from the beginning and are still my biggest fan, Love you Mum!

Emma Morrissey

United Kingdom

Website: www.emzportraitscrafts.wordpress.com

ISBN: 978-0-9926276-3-8

British Library Cataloguing-in-publication Data
A catalogue record for this book is available from the British Library

Cover design and inside Artwork by Emma Morrissey
Printed and bound in Great Britain by Lulu.com

This is an Advice book and should in no way be used as a replacement for business start-up, or legal advice.

Acknowledgements:

Mum! You have been my biggest supporter all my life, thanks for being the best Mum in the world!

My Publishers at Aloejimmy Publishing - James Marsh and James Reeves, thank you for your continued support, its great working with you and you continue to inspire me. Jane Sibley for your support in the early days, David Vane and SBGN, Solent University/Solent Creatives and Nicky Curtis, Southern Entrepreneurs, Wildern school and the D.@rt Centre, Southampton Daily Echo, everyone at ETC Community Magazine, BBC Radio Solent and That's Solent T.V.
To anyone I have missed, please accept my apologies; A big, big Thank you to everyone who has supported me in my business, I couldn't do without you.

Painting the Picture of Business.

A Guide For Creative People Thinking About
Starting A Business.

By Emma Morrissey BA

Contents

Introduction:

Are you an Artisan?
Ever thought what it would be like to start a business using your artistic skill?
Whether you're an Artist, Photographer, Dancer or Graphic Designer; if you've ever thought about what it would be like to start your own business, then this is the book for you. With personal advice and tips from someone who has done it, this book will guide you through some of the elements to consider before making that all important decision.

Painting the picture of Business, a guide for creative people thinking about starting a business,

This book also has note pages and templates, which can act as your very own workbook; for you to start exploring your potential.
Emma Morrissey is a fine artist and business woman in the South of England, creating custom artworks and teaching Art and Enterprise, but like all small businesses she came across setbacks.
After hard work, determination and training, Emma pursued her dream and set up her business in 2014. Now Exhibiting across Hampshire and is now using her experience to help others, Emma decided to put her knowledge and experience into this book for you to explore your dreams.

Emma Morrissey

What is a business?

Well you can find it in your everyday life, from supermarkets, high-street stores to your favorite football team, all of these things that make up our lives are businesses, whether it be for our entertainment, special events or our everyday essentials, everything runs around it, a money making, time consuming machine.

Painting The Picture Of Business

Where It All Began

Since I can remember I have always loved art. According to my mum, I have been drawing since I could hold a pencil, everything from colouring books to painting whilst travelling on the train, it is something that's always been part of my life.

The influence of music has always been a big part of my life; I wanted to draw my idols, so that they would be right in front of me and would stay with me forever. From the age of thirteen, I did my very first portrait, of a film star, it was then that I saw I had a talent for capturing a person's likeness and personality in a portrait and I enjoyed the process, it was different to anything I had drawn before. As time went on through practicing, the person's soul and emotion would come to life in front of me. But how would I turn this into a business?

For many years, I continued drawing, practicing as often as I could, each new face started to come to life in front of me, each music or film star came with a new challenge but everyone who saw my work, admired it, which built my confidence. After a while, I started to think, well lots of Artists sell their work and some make millions each year, be it for a different subject matter and media but still, there has always been a growing interest in Art across all communities, from the people in awe, to the purely curious.

Emma Morrissey

Art has brought much delight and atmosphere to many people's lives, from brightening up a living room with a canvas painting, to visiting some of the homes of the great masters.
The world of Art has come a long way, many have moved from pen and paint, to a camera and industrial sculpture; many of our modern Artists produce conceptual works of art, from live art to shock art, many appealing to a contemporary theme which fuels our interest and skepticism, encouraging many of us to ask what is it? Is it Art? It has also brought art back into the mainstream in a new, conceptual way which encourages us to challenge and ask questions.

My world of Art has stayed very traditional, with my preferred mediums staying much the same as they did over a decade ago, I guess you could say I like the production of creating a piece of art, starting with a blank canvas and ending up with a work that I may or may not have expected to be staring back at me.
So when you want to transform a hobby into a business where do you start? Well, the very beginning is when you know people are interested, by their compliments, it is often good to get feedback from strangers as they may be more likely to give you honest opinions and have no reason to be envious so therefore you get a more constructive idea of what someone may be willing to pay for your work, this can apply to artists, authors, photographers, jewelry makers, mostly any creative artisan, we all come under the same umbrella.

One of the first things to consider may sound obvious, but what will my business do? What is the reason for you starting

Painting The Picture Of Business

the business, is it to be financially independent? Is it to bring yourself into the community more, do you want to give your community more opportunities? Depending on whether you are an artisan, an author or a photographer, you will need to think about what your role in the business is; will you be a 'one man band' and handle all of the business aspects such as the 'Artistic' side, admin, meetings and finance, or will you have some help with those areas? As from my own experience as a 'one woman band' juggling the roles of Artisan, Administrator, Accountant and Front of House are all very challenging and you must remember to look after yourself and your personal wellbeing, as you are the business after all and can it function without you?

It is important to remember that there is only so much one person can do, if, like myself you take on more than one role in your business, than some of the tips in this book may be worth considering; but first, let's tell you a bit more about me. What makes me qualified to give such advice on business? Well apart from my personal experience as a business owner and taking on the role of artist, accountant, marketing manager and administrator, phew!
I have several qualifications which I studied for before starting my business, including qualifications in Business studies, Social Media, Marketing and Bookkeeping, I believe this, with my own experience gives me a good insight into how business can work for creative people who choose to go self-employed due to a lack of creative job roles available.

It is important to remember that I started the same way as most creative people do, with artistic experience and a dream, the rest you most likely will learn along the way, a lot of small businesses might work to a 'learning on the job' basis, this is ok, as no two peoples experience will be the same, each artist is different and what works for one might not for another, you can find your own strategies to learning the business side in a way that suits you. You may find that as you get to the business advice in this book, ideas might pop into your mind, you will find pages for notes and templates at the back of this book to help you.

My portrait of Slash, Lemmy and Ozzy, in graphite on paper.

Painting The Picture Of Business

From the fresh age of fifteen years old, I started my studies in College part time, through hard work and creativity I built many skills, little did I know that such skills are needed to actually run a business, communication is something I found came naturally, learning several ways to communicate with various people from different backgrounds has helped me immensely.

From starting at college, through to completing my Foundation diploma in Art and Design, I had built a strong portfolio of Artwork in several mediums and themes, I was given my place in University at the age of nineteen, where I studied for my Degree in Fine Art for three years. One of my favored past times believe it or not was writing, from my University dissertation to making lists, these skills have become essential in helping me to run my own business. Despite being organized, you don't have to be to run your business, there are many people who run successful businesses who don't consider themselves organized at all, they focus on the main body of the business and may have an assistant or someone to help with the administrative side of business for them; so you may choose to get someone to do your book-keeping and correspondence for you.

Many businesses do this, some work in a partnership basis where someone may be the creator, making or producing the work and someone else making the appointments and filing important documents and receipts etc; it is often known as the front and back of house. This is important to keep in mind to know that there are ways of running a business if you make sure to find all the information you need before you start.

Emma Morrissey

After graduating from University I knew I wanted to start a business, unfortunately serious health setbacks put my endeavors on hold and with little advice on what to do after University; I didn't know where to go from there, I knew I wanted to sell my Artwork, as I had always had compliments on my work and people seemed interested which is important to know you have something that people want. The problem was that, I had no idea how businesses really worked or exactly what it involved.

The crash of employment from 2011 meant I was unemployed, which can be a disheartening time for most young people who have just obtained a qualification only to be knocked back by potential employers, during this difficult time and undergoing hospitals tests, I still managed to stay positive and with each job interview I went to, it was good experience for business, all things that you can think about, from dressing executively, to learning how to answer questions professionally, thinking outside the box and maintaining eye contact, all these interview techniques can be used in business, especially in the early days when you are networking with other businesses as the first impression is very important.

Painting The Picture Of Business

Pastel pencil drawing on black card of Marvel's Doctor Strange,

2017

Emma Morrissey

After many attempts in various job sectors with the skills I already had, something still didn't feel right and I knew that I had to look into Self Employment further; I embarked on a Business course, which would be the first step into broadening my mind and as I had already tried my hand at drafting a business plan of my own, I had ideas already on what I wanted to do, who my market could be and my business name.

The course covered areas like keeping track of your businesses finance, set up costs to consider, doing a personal survival budget, advertising and promotional items like business cards. I took as much from this as possible and also did a course in Customer Service which gave me a great insight into the best way to work with my customers and to make sure that I give them all the relevant information they need to make an informed decision.

This made me focus more into how I'm treated as a customer when I make a purchase in a shop, how does the sales assistant greet me? Are they helpful? Do they ask if you need anything else? How do you want to be treated as a customer? Thinking like this was very helpful as it gave me an idea of what to say to customers and to find out what they are looking for, is there something that I could offer a particular group pf people?

Within a year I had put together a detailed and concise business plan which had everything from my forecast set up costs to my target markets which I had defined through researching into current trends. I did a lot of market research and created surveys which I gave to several people; friends to

Painting The Picture Of Business

business owners, this gave me feedback on my business services and prices. After a year of research and study I felt ready to set up as Self Employed, registering it and had my first few sales which was a great feeling.

Over the next few pages, I will share more of my experiences and my top tips for anyone wanting to know more about business.

Emma Morrissey

Overcoming The Early Pitfalls.

It's important to remain humble in business, as an Artist it is important to stay open minded but remain loyal to your work, personally I have always had a passion for portraiture, although it may not have a conceptual theme to it, I knew that I wanted to carry on creating portraiture. You may be the only port of call for your customers, so it's not just the work your customers are buying, they are buying you as well.

Name Sake: - Having a solid business name is important to get noticed and you want something that people will remember you for and says something about the business and what it does. It is important to think of what you want your business to say, do you want it to directly advertise what you do? Some small businesses will have their name in the business, this can work for some businesses but may not work for others, depending on your position in the business will help you decide this.

If you are the business so to speak, the artist for example then having your name in the business may work, whereas if you are in a partnership with someone else then it may be both names, all this is worth dedicating some time to before you start, as you don't want to be stuck with a name that could make business difficult for you. Think about what sector your business falls into – Art/Illustrator, Photographer, Ballet Dancer, Vocalist, or Jewelry Maker; what part do you play in the business, are you the front of the business, the artisan, or do you handle the admin side of things?

Painting The Picture Of Business

I always believed that being honest and natural with your customers is the best way forward, because, if you think about it, yourself, as a customer, you know whether you are going to buy something from an assistant in a shop, or if you're not, for example; if the assistant is pushy or rude, this may make you feel pressured or uncomfortable, therefore you won't make the purchase and you'll go elsewhere; so by being yourself with your customers and making sure that they understand the process by ordering with you will help them to make that decision.

When buying a creative work of art in some form, it is important for the buyer to know how it's been made for them, especially if it's custom made, by sharing this with your customers, it gives the story to how the piece was born and formed, by involving the customer in that process, they can then make the decision for themselves when it comes to buying from you, without feeling pressured.

In the early days of business, you may come across some setbacks, this happens and it is important to try and look forward and not let it get you down. There have been times where you will spend hours preparing for a craft stall and after six hours, you won't have broken even, this can be very disheartening and make you rethink, thoughts like 'what am I doing?' 'I can't do this' may cross your mind in these moments.

Thinking can be helpful if it is for the future of your business, for example, if you have a dry patch in business, with little sales, or in really hard times, no sales, it is often useful to revisit your original business plan and update it to include newer market areas you can work towards to, as well as researching into current trends that may be the ticket you need to getting some customers.

However, over thinking can be destructive.

You are creative after all,

You don't want to kick yourself when you're down and you can't expect yourself to get it right the first time.

Emz Top Tip: - *If you experience a dry patch with little or no sales, window shop, taking notice of the window displays, what items are placed at the front? Where are the 'sale' items? Is there lighting on the window display? What height is it at? Also pay attention to what the customers are buying. Create some more market research surveys with more specific questions to get some detailed feedback from potential customers.*

Another great way to get feedback from people when your business is struggling is to attend some networking events, this can be a great way of getting inspired by other business owners who have been in the same position you have and by surrounding yourself with other business people, it can help you to think in a business way, which could lead to some new ideas for your business.

Emz Top Tip: - *It is worth researching your local Networking groups, some of these may run networking breakfasts or day events which include business stands and seminars, it is worth looking for something similar in your area as most of these are run in hotels and have free admission. Check your local Business Newspaper for listed opportunities.*

Painting The Picture Of Business

My Business advertised in a local Magazine April 2015.

I did a lot of research into my industry and how my craft could work as a business; I did Business taster days, training and market research, to define if going self-employed would be plausible and the important must haves in business like tax, customer service and sales; even watching T.V series that focus on business had its helpful parts as it got me thinking in a business way.

Being a creative person and turning that from a hobby to a business is very challenging as there is no set of rules or a special uniform for you to wear when you go to work each day, for some people, this can bare a problem, as they may not feel like they are doing a 'job' so some people, be it a painter, sculptor or card maker, may decide to wear a suit when they go to business meetings, or getting their business logo printed onto a t-shirt, even if it is to discuss a painting commission, as it can put you in the mind-set of wearing a uniform, if that helps.

Going self-employed was a big decision for me, one that I spent over a year researching and training before I made my final decision, I can't state enough the importance of that, the more Market Research you do to find out where you would sit in your industry, prepares you and gives you an honest look at the situation.

You may need to have a part time job to help whilst you start your business, you may decide that you're not ready, or that your business wouldn't make enough money and that your business idea may need to be re-worked; I hope that this book will help give you some of the facts and situations you may face.

Many businesses have advisors, on business in general, customer relations and to profit margins+, sometimes you find that your business isn't going to make you money and may be better off as a community group or on a voluntary basis or charity, all these options are good to look into, it is also good so you know that even if your business won't be financially variable, you may still have your idea realized just in a different context. Researching into your options early is a wise as it could stand you in good stead when it comes to business being feasible. Here are some areas worth researching into further.

Premises: - If your business needs a premises then it's worth looking early, even just to get an idea for the current price rates, you may be able to find an empty shop available or an

Painting The Picture Of Business

office in a business center to rent, this might be worth researching if you need an office space to do marketing or to keep up to date on the finance for example.

Non for profit: - If you decide that your business could work well as a non for profit idea than it may be worth looking into Charites and community organizations.

Drawing from experience: What does it all mean   for a Creative in the industry?

Since 2010 there has been an considerable increase in Self-Employment due to the lack of jobs and an increase in 0 hour contracts as well as the new 'millennial' generations possibly going self-employed. Self-Employment is also a very popular choice amongst creative people, as many often go into freelance work, it is becoming much harder to find work within our fields, from Fashion to Graphic Designers, it also allows for flexibility for creative people who have other jobs and family as you are the boss and therefore you can create the hours that suit you. Self-Employment is also very popular amongst single Mums, as it allows some flexibility around busy home life.

As I mentioned earlier, some people may wear a suit for certain events but I have also found it very helpful to create a timetable, which can allow you to allocate certain time to each area of your business, which helps to get things organized and therefore get work done without getting too bogged down.
Artisans and creative people could include:
- Artist/Illustrator
- Performing Arts – Dancer, Singer, Actor
- Author

Emma Morrissey

- Photographer, Model
- Fashion Designer
- Animator

And many, many more.

These talented people are more likely to be self-employed, in order to use their passions and skills to their full potential by creating jobs for themselves; either by having a shop or hiring themselves on a freelance basis to a company. Unlike the conventional jobs, some self-employed people may have several people who they work for on a freelance basis, much like builders or plumbers. As long as you have passion for what you do and have done your research, running your own business is a very soul warming experience and it is the best decision I ever made. However, self-employment isn't for the faint hearted, it takes dedication and the ability to stick with it, as you will often find yourself working more hours than you would working in a store, you may find that in the very beginning you will be spending more time on the advertising part of your business than doing the creative work because you have to spend a certain amount of time getting the word out there and setting up.

Most of us artisans may decide to work from art studios where we can work as long as we like, so you have to be strict with yourself to make sure you give yourself 'Me' time, as this is crucial to allow yourself time to refuel and rebuild your creative flow which can be worn down by long hours. It make sense to think through your options before you take the plunge, if you decide to go for it, getting things rolling may take time to start with.

Painting The Picture Of Business

You could decide to join a creative group, a simple idea but you'd be surprised the tips it may give you. If you have a creative business idea, you will need all the creative people around you to help motivate you; signing up to local clubs and keeping an eye on activities in your area will give you an idea of what's trending; is painting more popular in one area than another? Is there a strong photographic society near you? Are there competitions you could enter? All these things could be potential market research for your business and confidence boosters.

It is also worth considering visiting local creative venues, music venues for example and observing, how does it work? Who looks after that aspect of it? These sorts of questions apply to all businesses, as each business will need people at front and back of house, in music terms, think of the back of house like a lighting, set, or think of a drummer in a band, keeping the beat going throughout, assisting the others with their timing and the front of house being the lead singer, the person that people think of because they see them first or see them the most? There are many roles that apply in business and in large businesses, many, the core ones will apply to you as well, finance officer, accountant, marketing assistant and of course, the directors, managers and the owner of the business.

Profit:- This can be a difficult part of any business, especially as most businesses don't feel the benefit of a profit until there third year of operation, when it comes to creative businesses, that it most definitely the case.

Observe and Learn: - Taking the time to observe is very important, from watching adverts on T.V, looking at adverts

Emma Morrissey

in directories to bill boards. Pay attention to the information given, how much is there? Does it grab your attention?

Pay attention to market sellers when you visit a market stall, whether it be for food or beauty products, how do they talk to you, do they approach you straight away? Do you feel pressured, what attracted to their stall? All these things can help you to think about how you will approach your own customers, some approaches work with some customers, some like to get into a conversation and some don't, some just want to talk and have no interest in buying at all so this is where reading people can be helpful as you can think 'do they need time to look at the products first or do I jump straight in?

Dancing Through Life.

Performing Arts, whether it be through dance, vocals or drama. Performing Arts has a great way of helping many of us express ourselves in various ways through a medium that we can respond to, many performances, even when in mime can evoke such emotion that it is something we all strive to, even just by watching our favorite actors in films.

All of our idols would most likely have done some form of Performing Arts or Musical theatre in their early careers, giving us the inspiration and motivation we need to try it for ourselves, with many ballroom dance classes being taken across the U.K through the popularity of recent Television shows and other forms of exercise such as yoga being used in meditative therapies, it is easy to see why we are so taken by this form of energetic expression.

So what do you do if you're in the Performing Arts industry and thinking of setting up your own business, you might want

Painting The Picture Of Business

your own dance company to train young dancers, or you may want to offer your skills to companies on a freelance basis, as a stand-in perhaps, well, here is a bit more about my Performance background; for many years have included vocals in my everyday life, with a passion for several styles of music and vocal technique I live everyday through it, varied from ballads to melodic heavy metal, and dance has also played a large part of my life through live performances and grueling rehearsals.

Social Media: Using YouTube is a great tool for any performer, as it acts as a live platform to showcase dancers, singers and actors work and get feedback, remember that many celebrities have been found through YouTube by producers and recording companies so having your work out there is a must for any performer.

Having platforms on Twitter and LinkedIn is worthwhile, as well as thinking of which platforms are best for you, you may benefit from a bog, or if you're an artist/photographer then Pinterest or Snapchat may be worth thinking about, having a Facebook page for yourself as a performer can give you the all-important exposure you need to build likes and activity. LinkedIn is a must for any business person, whether you're part of a company or freelance, as setting up your profile, listing your skills and education in the arts, there are also a lot of different groups you can join on LinkedIn which can broaden your range and get you networking with other performers and companies looking at hiring performers. It is also worth knowing that keeping things simple and professional in a stills portfolio is best, whether you have photos on black or with paper with a small caption is best unless you've been asked specifically for something different.

21

Emma Morrissey

It is worth researching current C.V's and Statements of performers as this can be a good idea when applying for a live role, sometimes a simple creative pattern can be effective and elegant enough to stand out as opposed to having a C.V that is very fussy and hard to read as a result. Remember to keep to the most relevant and impressive experience on the first page, as you want to encourage the reader to read on, C.V's are traditionally a maximum of two pages long. Include all performance and study experience and events you have performed in as well as having a clear and creative introduction.

When studying or using a space such as a stage, it is worth setting up a camera and filming or getting someone to film it for you, put together a collection of your best performances to act as your digital portfolio for potential employers to see your skill.

Portfolio: This is worth having in two formats, a live portfolio for film of your performances, either available on a C.D or U.S.B, as well as making sure you have an accessible channel on YouTube or Vimeo for potential companies to look at your work, but it is also important to have a stills portfolio, which gives the company the opportunity to see how your performance looks in a still frame, which could lead to photoshoots and other further exposure. Have a range of different styles in your portfolio, to show your versatility and ability to adapt.

Painting The Picture Of Business

Screenshot from one of my short dance films entitled 'Hurt'

2011.

Emz Top Tip: - *You can get professional portfolio folders from all good stationers and Arts and Crafts shops.*

Auditions: So, you're a freelancer, about to do an audition for a company, where do you start? Breathe, plan ahead, rehearse as much as you can but remembering to rest before your audition so that you're in good shape with rested limbs. Sleep is a must to ensure you are well rested and refreshed ready for your audition. It is important to remember that from your portfolio, both live and stills, that a company will want to see your range and ability when performing.

Emma Morrissey

Food is also important, as you don't want to feel faint before your audition, so stick to something light and full of fiber, slow releasing to keep away the hunger. It is also important to eat afterwards, again, stick to something light, but nourishing to replace any lost fluids such as sweat. It might help to make notes of what your audition piece is, how long etc., just to give you something to look over before you start, this can help to avoid the fear of going blank when it's time for your audition.

It is worth remembering to use as much of the space you have as possible, keeping in mind that you want all the panelists to be able to see you and give as much eye contact as you think necessary.

Rehearsals: Rehearsals are often the one thing most dancers anticipate the most. As it can take hours of dedication and perfection to master, from perfect unison, to cannon effects, it is important to remember that dancers all learn at different levels and it is important to remain patient, it is often the one simplest step combination that may stump you, so taking regular breaks and making time to drink plenty of water is a must, to regulate yourself and reserve much needed energy.

Vocalists – The standard warm ups are good, it is important to find out if there is a set of songs to choose from or can you do your own piece? Don't overstretch your vocals as you want your voice to be at its best ready to wow the audition, so rest your voice the night before and drink plenty of water. Use special effect only when necessary to avoid overdoing the

Painting The Picture Of Business

vocal, try to show your range in this audition. Use as much space as you can, giving eye contact if required.

Dancers – Get plenty of rest the evening before, with a good night's sleep, before your audition, warm up your muscles with stretches and light exercise, you don't want to go for it and pull something at the last minute! Use as much space as you can, giving eye contact.

Actors – Warm up your vocals with simple exercises, warm up your muscles as well. Use as much space as you can, giving eye contact.

Research: It may be well worth trying to find out who is on the panel of judges for your audition and the venue's history to help you to familiarize yourself, as well as being prepared if they ask any questions about the company, there is nothing worse than being asked about the company you are auditioning for and not knowing what to say, sometimes you can get so overwhelmed by focusing on the content and timing of your audition that you forget the all-important company research.

Hire Charges: This can be difficult, as how do you put a price on performance? It is worth researching into the going rates for dancers, actors and vocalists, do they charge by the hour, by the day or is there a set rate with the company?
Now to be honest, many of us spend a lot of our time creating work and may not be seen outside in the world for several days at a time completing work as a hobby; but in business, the only way to get customers is to get out there and speak to people, networking is an important element in all business owners arsenal, so here we go!

Emma Morrissey

The Art of Networking.

Networking can be challenging to start with, more so if you aren't the chatty type, but remember that you are talking about you, what you do and what you plan to do and everyone else is there for the same reason, to create contacts and build knowledge of the local business area. It is worth looking at your local networking groups and if you contact the organizer, ask how the attendance is, some do charge for breakfast networking for example.

The one thing to remember is that you are just starting out and therefore you can't expect yourself to be an expert, but you can talk to other business owners and soak up the atmosphere, this can be quite inspiring and give you the all-important motivation in the early days.

It is also good experience to get yourself used to thinking of yourself in a business sense and showcasing what your business has to offer, this is helpful if you are asked to do a presentation or business introduction for example, this is often known as a 'pitch'.

Emz Top Tip: - *It may sound obvious but, remember to bring plenty of business cards and fliers with you when attending networking meetings and events, don't be afraid to give someone a business card, even if they don't ask for one..*

Painting The Picture Of Business

Myself on a panel at a University.

Emz Top Tip: - *Make a list of important notes about your business when you attend a networking meeting,, you may get nervous so having some notes to hand will help you when introducing yourself.*

Elevator Pitch:- This is a term you will come across a lot when you start to do some research, this is basically your selling pitch when you meet with business owners or introduce yourself as a new business, this is a concise and positive view of you and what you do, in some networking groups, you may be asked to do a x30 second pitch, this can be quite taxing but it is actually a great way of sifting through

Emma Morrissey

all of your information from your USP (Unique Selling Point) to what you offer and condensing it down into the most essential points which will interest your group of potential customers.

Business Dress Code: - For networking groups, most people dress formally in a suit or smartly dressed, so best to leave the trainers at home!

Being Interviewed on T.V in 2016

Painting The Picture Of Business

However there are some times where you can mix and match, known as smart casual, smart shoes or flats, in a dark colour, most people tend to favor black or navy, put with a simple smart pair of trousers/skirt could be worn with a simple top if it's not essential to wear a shirt and a jacket or cardigan, you can inject a bit of colour in there if you like, you are an Artisan after all. In some events where it is important for you to be seen as an Artisan, especially when you get more confident with these sort so networking groups and meetings.

Seminars: - If you decide to hold a seminar at a networking or business event, it's worth researching into your subject matter for the seminar, is it mainly to promote your business? Promote a new product? Whatever your seminar is based around, it's helpful to research tips and promotional materials you may want to give away of offer at the seminar, for example, money off vouchers, free pens etc.

Presentations: - When creating a PowerPoint presentation, you may need to make a list of what you wish to cover in the presentation, allowing for questions and answers at the end. You may use que cards to help keep you on track when talking through your presentation.

Emz Top Tip: - *Make bullet points for your presentation and figure out your order of subjects.*

Emma Morrissey

Market your business.

What is marketing? Marketing is the television adverts you see during seasonal times of the year and food promotions, posters on the side of buses and at bus shelters, famous actors in television advertisements, all these are a way of marketing a product or service, by appealing to us through good marketing strategy.

Many of the established companies in the world, have specialist people doing the marketing campaigns for them, a group of people who make us aspire to be more glamourous, more technically minded or work harder to achieve our dream car or dream purchase. All this is achieved through marketing.

My Business logo.

Some of us may even do this in daily life without even knowing it. If you are part of a dating site or enjoy meeting new people, you will no doubt, post all of your best qualities, as it's true you never get a second chance to make a first impression, so by sharing the best and most relevant things about yourself on friend profiles online, you are actually marketing yourself; in the best way, the same applies for businesses and this is how you let people know about your latest offer or new product/service.

Painting The Picture Of Business

Logos: - Having a logo, something that sets you apart and looks better than just a name on a page, if you're a photographer, it might be an image from a photoshoot that you feel sums up your business, if you're a dancer, it might be a still shot of you dancing on stage. You can create your own logos on programs such as Word and other websites online for free.

Tagline: - A tagline is another term for a phrase, having a phrase can be a great way of getting people to remember your business, you'll notice even when you watch adverts, most of the big companies will have a catchy phrase or jiggle attached to it, which people then associate with that business, it is a good way to get recognized and remembered. This may often be a short phrase or a saying, which may say something about what your business does as a service or the type of products you sell, or it could be based around the customer service. You can then implement this onto business cards, flyers and more.

Marketing your business is the most important part of your business after actually setting up, as it puts you and your business on the map, whether it be through fliers, your website or regular updates on twitter.
It is worth researching how similar businesses market themselves and decide what will work for your business, it's worth looking into the price of local articles to advertise your business as well as asking around for the best deal to help promote your business, most community magazines will want to support local businesses so this can be a good place to start.

Emma Morrissey

First of all, you need to think, what am I doing this marketing for? What is my objective? Is it to gain sales? Is it to build business contacts? Or is it to create business awareness? You may want all of these, but bear in mind that the marketing approach for each may need to be different. If, like many creative people and are sole trade, you may find yourself doing most of your marketing and promotional work online, either through email, social media or blogs, so what to do when your internet goes and you have a deadline to meet?

Emz Top Tip: - *Save all your updated work on a memory stick as often as you possibly can, remember there are local libraries and Wi-Fi hot spots which you can use to research and can easily save an image or email text to yourself to pick up in one of these places, that way you can add it to your project until your interest is fixed.*

Advertising: Think about the types of advertising you are most likely to use, Things like: - Radio, Magazines/Newsletters. Using signs may be another good way of advertising your business, you may notice when you are out and about that many cars and vans advertise their business on their vehicles, with the business name, number and social media links, this can be a good way of letting people know what you do just by driving around.

Emz Top Tip: - *If you do plan on getting a car/van sign made for you, make sure you find out all legal requirements for this before you do it!*

Painting The Picture Of Business

You can also get special holders and stands for any posters, leaflets and business cards, you can get these from all good stationers and come in a range of styles and sizes.

Emz Top Tip: - *Some stationers and Printing companies can produce a pull out banner for you, these can be available in various sizes from table top banners to 8 foot tall pull out banners, these are great for business launch campaigns and display stands where you want to create an impact and allow people to see your stand from afar.*

A photo from Teaching at one of my Art Classes

Emma Morrissey

Promotional material/freebees?
You may see these in shops or authorizations, they may have their business printed onto pens, pencils, notebooks; another good way of you advertising your business and giving something to potential customers when building business awareness.

Clothing: - You'll notice that many of the shops you go into, the assistants will have either a uniform or a t-shirt with the business name and logo printed on it, this is also good as it helps you to identify who works there, you may see some wearing name tags or badges, which may have their job title, such as assistant manager or sales advisor.

Emz Top Tip: - *There are many t-shirt printing services available where you can get your business printed onto garments and you can easily create your own name or ID badge using Word or other programs.*

Tailored Emails/Letters:
Sending tailored emails can be a good way to get your business in front of influential people in business, whether it be to advertise your business for you on their blog, to having a small space in their shop/venue to display your work. It is worth going through your directory to look for local places and people who may be interested in either buying your products/service or promoting it for you, make a list of these and start contacting them. Here's an example:

Painting The Picture Of Business

To whom it may concern/F.A.O. For attention of - (Use this if you know the person's name.)

I'm a local business owner in ..... and I'd like to introduce myself to you, I specialize in .... and I was wondering if you would be interested in my product/service as I believe it would be a great asset to your venue.

I would greatly appreciate the opportunity to work with you.

Regards,

(Sign)

Email Signature: - An email signature is a good way of telling the recipient who you are and what you do, this can work in a way of letting the person know that you are serious about sending your emails. You can also add a link to your business website or social media page which could allow the recipient to view what you do and offer. If you have a Gmail account you can add your own signature to the end of your emails, you can usually find this in settings.

Press Release: - A press release does exactly what it says on the tin. A press release is a piece of writing that you would give to someone to let them know exactly what it is you do and who you are and when you are introducing a new product, service or an event. You may be asked to do these when submitting to a magazine, you can find many examples on how to write one online. Here is an example:

Emma Morrissey

Press Release:
Business Name:
Business Owner:
Explain what your business does in a couple of sentences,
include the service/product, your sale strategy, who in the
market are you aimed to. Mention a few latest achievements,
this could be getting a spot on radio or in your local
newspaper/or art event about to land in your local
community with artists, charity tombola, face painting etc.

<u>Cold Calling:</u> - Now this is usually something that everyone hates, because we all hate having our time wasted but it some cases, it can be the main way you generate interest in your business. The way to start this is by making it clear who you are and what you do and who you'd like to talk to, chances are they say they're not interested but if you start out with honesty, you may encourage honesty in return. You may find some venues that you know would benefit from using your service or having your products in their shop/premises, here's an example:

"Hi There, My name is ... and I was wondering if I could talk
to your events manager? I'm a local business owner and I
was wondering if you could give me some advice as I believe
that my products may be of interest to you, I'd appreciate
your time."

Emz Top Tip: - *Remember all they can say is no and for every ten*
you contact, one might say yes and you don't know if that one
person might be a potential long lasting customer of yours.

36

Painting The Picture Of Business

<u>Monthly Reviews:</u> - It can be a good idea to put something in place so you can review how your business is performing, some businesses already do this by their stock take for example, which gives them direct feedback on what item is selling well and therefore needs restocking and which aren't doing so well.

Emz Top Tip: - *It is important to put together a monthly timetable so you can review how your business is going at the end of each month.*

Magazine article about my business in April 2015.

Emma Morrissey

Emz Top Tip: - *Set up Google Alerts or buy your local paper – Setting up Alerts for news items to be emailed straight to you i.e. – Photography in Wiltshire*

<u>Just Ask:</u> - Being brave enough to ask advice is a great way to get acquainted with business people and show that you are not afraid to ask questions, at the end of the day, the worst thing you can hear is 'No'. This can apply to asking to have a small space in someone's shop window, to a small advert in a magazine or newspaper, if you ask around the community sectors you might be able to get articles for a reasonable price or better. It is important to network and take part in business events to get your face out there as well as your work.

Emz Top Tip: - *It is worth looking at local courses in P.C programs, especially if you're going to be using software such as Microsoft and more, some courses are reasonable and will give you an insight into using such programs effectively, this can be very helpful if you're going to be doing most of your marketing on a computer.*

<u>Radio:</u> - Some local radio stations also advertise local events for free or a small fee so this may be a good way of reaching several hundred people in your area about a specific event you will be attending, whether it be a craft stall at Christmas or an exhibition in a local gallery. Craft stalls is a good option for many artisans, whether you are a card maker, an Artist, photographer or an author as there are many stalls both indoors and out, outdoors is popular for artists and sculptors who may need more space to display their work to potential customers.

Painting The Picture Of Business

<u>Other promotional material:</u> - *It is well worth you getting some professional photographs of yourself taken, these can be used on your social media platforms profile pictures and ID cards and are a great way of showing people, you, the business owner, this is also helpful when connecting with other business owners and meeting up at a networking meeting, this way you have an idea what the person looks like.*

<u>Website blogs.</u> - Mostly all companies and venues hold events of some sort, this could be for community day activities, craft fayres or business meeting rooms; this is a good way for the company to bring in extra money, reach more people and work with other businesses. If you have an event coming up, it may be worth asking your local community websites or local council if they have a page dedicated to local events, this could be a way of getting your event advertised to more people.

Emma Morrissey

A Christmas Craft stall 2014.

Emz Top Tip: - *It's worth researching your local craft stalls online or by looking in local newspapers for upcoming events which may be a good opportunity to sell your work.*

Creating posters and Signs: - It is important to remember not to confuse or overwhelm the customer with too much information, so use bold and clear fonts of text that can be easily read, using short, catchy sentences that say only the most relevant information.

Emz Top Tip: - *When designing a poster or sign for a new product/service, test it on yourself and friends, get them to walk past it and see if it catches their eye or grabs their attention, if it doesn't why doesn't it? Sometimes the simplest of changes can make all the difference.*

Painting The Picture Of Business

Getting Customers

What is a customer? Or consumer as we are also known, everyone is a potential customer, even the owners of big business companies are customers to someone, the stock dealers they buy from, the supermarkets they get their evening meals from, the brand of clothing they wear, but in business you may come across the term 'clients' as this can sound more professional. Once you have found the type of people who would benefit from the product or service you offer, you can begin to market to them, this is called your 'Target Market'.

Recommendations: - From your first few sales it is a good idea to ask your past customers if they could give you their feedback or a recommendation, people will often think more about doing business with you if you can show evidence of the work you've done for customers before, this could be through social media websites or follow up emails with your customers and documenting their feedback on your website.

Emz Top Tip: - *If you ask for feedback from a customer, make sure you ask for their permission to post their feedback online.*

Emma Morrissey

Prices and what do I charge?

This has its tricky parts, we often find ourselves at opposite ends of the spectrum, as we see value in our work as we are the creators; so are we asking too much for it? Or are we underselling ourselves by not seeing the true value? Getting this right is one of the hardest parts of pricing, it's important to remember that you can easily reduce prices, but it is not so easy to put prices up.

In the terms of illustrators for example, many will begin by calculating the cost of the materials, charge a price for their time per hour and the total is the total they charge their customers. Some businesses will charge hourly or per day. In these cases, companies will have set prices for certain products or services, working on the idea of, you get what you pay or if you pay more for something, you should, ideally, get more for the money? Whether that be in terms of more products or better quality that warrants the price tag, this is for you to decide where your business lies, is it the quality or the quantity? There can be benefits to both, the trick is finding which fits your business best.

Emz Top Tip: - *Research what your competitors are charging for similar services/products, how much you need in order to cover your costs for creating the product/service and how much would you pay yourself as your salary, then add it together and consider your mark up, 205% of the amount for example, to get your AVO (Average Value Order) price, this is what you can quote to a customer..*

Painting The Picture Of Business

Calculating your costs:

Calculating your costs can be difficult in terms of valuing your time if that is the main area of price, but if you create a product then start by calculating how much your materials cost you to buy, for example, canvasses and paints, tools/equipment. Then add your time, what you're left with is your cover costs, this is the cost you need to make back to break even when selling your product/service, then figure out how much profit you want to make on each order, even if you only make 10% on each order in the beginning, this is good, any profit is still profit, consider a percentage on top of the cover costs, this is known as mark up. Example – A company buyssome beauty products 'Wholesale' for £2.50 each, they then sell them to the customer for £5.00 each, which is a 50% mark up. Remember that you may not see your profit in the early years, as the majority of your first year or two will be taken up in your startup costs like, materials, premises and promotional items.

For example, your cost to create a commissioned painting including your materials and time = £100, this is the cost you need to make in order to break even, so if you sell your painting for £120, you have made a small profit, if you end up selling it for £85 then you haven't broken even and this could affect the likelihood of making a profit by the end of the tax year. Ways to avoid having to sell at a loss is to consider asking for a deposit on custom products/services, this is the basic amount you need to cover your costs or a small percentage, this can ensure that you won't be out of pocket if the commission falls through.

Emma Morrissey

For example, a commissioned piece costs you £100 and you are going to charge £200, getting the deposit of £100 in advance, covers your costs and also lets you know how committed the customer is. It is also worth testing your friends and family on your price drafts or, do some market research surveys with some draft prices and ask them to pick which one they would be most willing to pay for the product or service you offer, this is a way of testing if your prices are too high, too low or about right.

Where are my customers?

So you've done your market research, you know who your target market is, you've had some business exposure; so how do you get customers and commissions?

Emz Top Tip: - *It is well worth looking into your local courses, you may find many business related courses available like sales, customer service and accounting.*

With a creative business, whether you are a card maker or a painter, be prepared for some of your work to be seasonal, as paintings, jewellery and cards for example will get more interest in the autumn months leading up to Christmas. This is a good opportunity to look at craft fayres as these are becoming more and more popular with recent T.V series demonstrating seasonal gifts you can make at home, that are both fun to make and unique items, we all desire to have something that is unique and shopping channels can fuel this. Invoice: - What is an invoice? An invoice is a document sent to someone who needs to make a payment, you may have had or seen these when ordering something online for example as

Painting The Picture Of Business

an invoice may be sent along with the product when it's delivered.

When a customer is ordering from you it may be a good idea to send them an invoice, if you accept card payments through your website via PayPal for example, this may be part of the ordering process, but you can find good templates online for invoices you can edit using Word or Excel. For cash payments received, you can buy invoice books from stationers, which include inked sheets which copy the details for you to keep a copy. You can get books in:

- Receipts
- Invoice

Plus many more, most businesses will use 'duplicate' books, these have say i.e. 100 sheets in sets of two, you give the original copy to the customer and the other is kept recorded for your records, this is recorded through a dummy ink sheet which comes with each book, it is good to keep these to keep track of your sales which can help you when updating your cash flow spreadsheet and for giving customers when you're dealing in cash sales.

Getting Payments: - This is often the part that many businesses find difficult when it comes to getting a customer to pay, some businesses offer their services/products with several instalment payments, this makes it more affordable for the customer, as well as keeping the business slowly flowing with regular money which can be very helpful if you have a dry month.

Many businesses will employ an accountant to send invoices to the businesses customers and in some cases, reminders and arrears. It is good to discuss payments with the customer when the order has been agreed, not only for both you and the

Emma Morrissey

customer fully knowledgeable on the process but it allows you
the opportunity to document when payments are due and if
your customers are up to date with paying.

In the case of cash payments, many businesses handle in cash
as it gives instant payment and you receipt cash payments
through receipt books and invoices as I mentioned earlier, this
will not only allow you to record your businesses income but
it will give your customers a record as well which can be very
reassuring when you are paying in cash.

Commission- Art portrait for a customer 2015.

Sales Aftercare: - Any follow up you have with your
customers that have bought from you, from a thank you email
for their custom, asking for feedback on the service they
received or offering them future discounts and special offers if
they give you more custom. It is important to keep your

Painting The Picture Of Business

customers in the loop as your business develops but make sure
they are ok with continued correspondence as you don't want
to run the risk of becoming a nuisance.

Craft Fayres:

What is a craft fayre? Craft Fayres come in all shapes and
sizes, from small venues inside with a few stalls selling
anything from market goods such as jams and cakes to full
scale fayres in, or outside with hundreds of stalls, they can
focus on certain themes, from arts and crafts which could
involve artwork, accessories, to bespoke furniture and vintage
clothes. You can find them all year round in various places up
and down the U.K and some are based seasonal times of the
year, such as Christmas and Easter.

Raffles: - A raffle is a prize draw where all of the craft fayre
stall holders will donate a product to the raffle as a prize, this
is a great way to show what you and the business does, make
sure you put a business card and a flier with the product!

So how do you haggle, well from a customer's point of view
it is a good way of getting the desired price and getting a
bargain, for the seller, it can be enjoyable as long as you know
the bottom price you must not exceed in order to still break
even and hopefully make a small profit on each product you
are selling.

Emz Top Tip: - *When haggling with a customer, start your price
higher rather than lower, this gives you a good spectrum for leeway.
Knowing that the customer will bring down your price gives them a
bargain and you, the price you need. So if you know you must get*

Emma Morrissey

*£10.00 at the lowest for a product, pitch at £20.00 making it clear
that you will come down slightly, this will ensure that your customer
doesn't just walk off and you lose a sale; if they do start to move on,
you can sell at £15.00 by meeting the customer half way, they've got
your price down by £5.00 and you have made a £5.00 profit.*

SALE!

Sales:
Having a sale can be a good way of encouraging new
customers to your stall and making room for new stock. It
may be the case that your reduced prices only reflect the cost
of producing them, meaning you have had to eliminate your
profit, but you may sell in bulk and if you do, you can still
draw the customers attention to your full prices items, if they
like it enough, they will buy it regardless of its full price tag.

Emz Top Tip *– Items you want to sell most place at prime eye
level to the customer with lighting on it, you can get leveling shelves
for tables that create height; this can create an attractive display
with levels for each item*

Online Shops:
What is it and what are the benefits of it? Well, you'll find
that many of your top high street stores also have an online
shop for their customers, so you can browse and purchase
items at your convenience. This is particularly beneficial if
you work during the daily shopping opening hours and don't
have time to make the shops and don't fancy braving the
crowds over the weekend to get the latest offers.

Painting The Picture Of Business

Online shopping has changed the way we shop, how and when we do it; shopping for food, clothes or furniture is now at our fingertips and gives us the opportunity to buy 24 hours a day and with some shops delivering to your door the very next day, it is no wonder that this is becoming the modern way to shop with no fuss.

If you don't have the opportunity to have your own shop or display space for your works then it might be worth researching into the cost of having an online shop. Many platforms offer business owners the chance to display images of their items for a small fee and the chance to create a personalized online shop page on the website, many of these websites offer the customer the chance to pay via PayPal which is a trusted and secure way of paying for items, so this might be well worth looking into.

If you are able to have a shop or just a space in a local venue and have products that are considerable in price, you can buy hand held card machines so you can accept card payments, this is called a 'Merchant Account', remember that these work best when a mobile phone signal can be obtained.
 This can be a unique way of obtaining more sales, particularly if you do a craft fayre that has a lot of interest from shoppers; you may find this if the craft stall is held near a shopping center where most shoppers purchase their items using a credit card and therefore may not carry a lot of cash which can lose you a potential sale. Merchant accounts do cost but there are lots of special offers available so it's worth looking at what you can get online.

Emma Morrissey

Emz Top Tip: - *It is worth looking when you are at a craft fayre to see if people are showing interest in buying items that are more costly or if they are carrying cash, if this is the case then your business may benefit from being able to accept card payments and may encourage potential customers to buy more.*

Craft fayres are a frequent activity for many artisans as they are a great way to show your products and mix with other crafters, however, it can be a stress getting all products packaged and ready when travelling to one early in the morning, so it is best to plan ahead, thinking, what am I going to bring? What are my latest products? How much am I going to charge? Do I have stock I can offer at a cheaper price to make room for my new items? It is also important to have a 'cash float' this is an amount of cash you will need if a customer gives you a note for example and you need to give change, this will ensue you don't lose a sale.

Emz Top Tip: - *Think of the best way to package your products so that they get to the destination safely and are easy to find when arranging your table display, you may want to think of using bags, boxes or travel cases for some larger items.*

Painting The Picture Of Business

Target Markets

Target Market, so what does that mean? Well, your target market is the key audience of people that could benefit most from your product or service, a lot of companies have a product in particular that they target to a particular audience for example, pretty much all restaurants will cater for children by having a set children's menu, which will notice may be written and designed in a colorful way with cartoon characters and activities for the child to do whilst they wait for their meal, so it's marketed in the best way.

It's possible that your business may provide several services or products and therefore you may have a few different target markets, for example, families, dog walkers or the night life, the more specific you can be when thinking about who would benefit from the product or service, the better you will be able to get sales by getting your product in front of the right people. You may need a separate strategy for each of your areas, for example, for a photographer, advertising with fliers at a local parent and toddlers group may be a good option, offering discounts for photoshoots.

Researching into your product and exactly what it does and what it 'brings to the party' so to speak, will help you to create a more specific sales pitch, as creative people, we produce our art or whatever our product might be, a photograph collection or even a dance routine for a company in a theatre, but it's interesting how often we really don't consider who will want it, yes, it is true that everyone could benefit from a product in some way but that doesn't help you, you need to be more specific and think what makes you go to certain shops, is it the price, is it the label? You will find that all the big high-street shops start in the same way we will, with a marketing strategy, who will what their product?

So think, what does your customer look like, what type of job do they do? For example, their budget will have a lot to do with where they shop, but it is good to remember that creative people are selling a desire not a necessity, everyone needs bread and milk so that's a must have, but not necessarily needs a painting? This is where marketing your business to the right people is essential.

Once you have done some market research and researched who your target markets are, it is important to put them into a timeline, how many do you have and importantly, how many of them are feasible in the beginning, as it might be the case that some of them you will be able to market to when your business has built up some credibility and earned some money as some marketing campaigns might be more costly and time consuming than others, so it is important to remember that you can only do so much and starting with the 'here and now' is a good place to start.

If you potentially have six target markets areas but only three of them are feasible at the moment then you can start to plan a strategy and how you propose to get to them with your business product or service. This will take time but it is worth it as you don't want to rush a strategy and realize nine months into your business that something's a miss, so planning and researching into your market is essential for success and progression is often a slow start for all creative businesses but a slow progression is better than no progression isn't it?

Painting The Picture Of Business

<u>So have a think about what your Target Markets are:</u>

My Business is:
Who are my customers?
Where are they?
How can I get them?

Target Market 1.)
Target Market 2.)
Target Market 3.)

<u>Notes:</u>

Emma Morrissey

Displaying your work

Display, what is it?
What does it make you think of?
An Exhibition in London's Tate?
A local school's art class?

So how do you go about displaying your work, how do you
expect to get customers and your business to get known in
your local area if you don't show your products? Displaying
your works can be a tricky thing to do, as many galleries and
display spaces do charge a fair amount, but it is worth
researching into these venues as you need to find out if
indeed, you get what you pay for?
If you pay a certain amount, within your budget of course,
does the venue get a lot of interest and a lot of people through
the door? Will that give you some customers and
commissions? It's worth shopping around. It's well worth
visiting some local galleries, spaces and other opportunities
that currently have work displaying, talk to the venue owner,
find out the prices, take notice of how many people are
looking at the current display, is it getting interest?

Painting The Picture Of Business

Me and my Mum at the opening night of one of my Solo Art Exhibitions

2015.

Exhibitions are hard to find, especially if you live outside of London, however there are still many venues from libraries, non-chain shops and other venues with space that may be willing to display various works. Once you've done some research it's worth asking the price and making an offer, it's important to remember that the venue most likely doesn't want to have empty space and for the sake of making an offer, the worst that could happen is they say no.

If you are willing and able to pay the charge the venue has set, it might be worth researching to find out if previous people who have displayed work have charged an admittance fee or offering tickets with a price attached, this can have a certain exclusivity to it and can help you break even if you don't manage to sell any of your works. If you do charge an admittance fee or tickets then you could always offer

Emma Morrissey

something to your paying customers on opening night, there are many things to consider that you could offer, from money off vouchers to free gifts or a raffle to win one of the pieces on display, all this can make the ticket price more acceptable.

Things to consider when you are exhibiting your work;

Who is the work for?
Who will like the work most, is there a theme?
If the work is inspired by the area you live in then it might be worth you inviting the local community authority figures in some way.

Emz Top Tip: - *Leave a comments book for the exhibition, it's a great way to get feedback from the public who are viewing your work and get a sense of if there is a lot of interest in it, this can help you when it comes to marketing your next exhibitions.*

So you've got your venue, you've agreed the price, how are you going to display it? In what order, what pieces? It is worth visiting some local galleries and paying attention to what pieces are displayed; what pieces are there, how are they spaced apart, what's the colour scheme? All of these things are worth taking note of as it can be the difference between a good exhibition display and a brilliant, eye catching exhibition.

Painting The Picture Of Business

Me, at one of my book signings – 2016.

My Artwork on display in Southampton, a collection of paintings in acrylic on canvas.

Emma Morrissey

Alone in the business world?

Being a business owner can feel lonely at times, especially if you work alone in the business as a sole trader. That's why attending local groups, networking and other business events is very important, not only does it get you out there in the world you've just embarked into, but it keeps you connected with others, which can be the ideal thing you need when your business comes to a standstill and you're struggling to move it forward.

Working with other business owners, can be nerve racking, but it is one of the most personally rewarding experiences as well as financially helpful for your business, it gives your business the potential to reach more customers and other businesses by sharing your skills and ideas.

This is also a great choice for creative business owners who work from their studios, an artist collaborating with other artists might be a good option for you, it gives you company, shared skills and means that creativity can flow as you all share the same passion.

I have had book covers published for a local author and this has been a great opportunity to share ideas and create something new with creative, inspiring people who share the same passion and motivation for their craft as you do.

Painting The Picture Of Business

Myself in the center, holding the authors book for launch in Kent. Left: James Reeves – Editor; Centre: Myself – Cover Artist; Right: James Marsh – Author.

Collaborating: - This is often something we don't think about, whether it be through fear of our ideas being shared without credit or fear of not knowing what to contribute. If you create work for customers or for the main collaborator, make sure you know exactly what part you play in the collaboration, how much work will you will doing? Can you do it with any other work commitments you have?

Emz Top Tip: - *Look at making contacts with business people who are looking to collaborate with others, either through networking events or online through social media. It may be worth talking about getting a contract drawn up or some form of document that stipulates what each person will be doing.*

Emma Morrissey

Contracts: - Having a contract can be very helpful in several business situations, from collaborations with businesses, to having a contract with customers who have made an order with you which is called an Invoice, this can protect you and your work, cover your production costs when making the work, whilst underlining who does what in a business collaboration. This could include copyright, who owns rights to what? To the money side of things.

Here's an example of a basic contract, with some of the elements you might want to include:

Contract:

Between .... and ...... (Name all the people involved.
What is the nature of this collaboration ......?
Rights and Copyright: ... (If you are an artist or photographer, will you still own the rights to use the images again or will they be effectively sold to the other person/people in this collaboration?)
Percentage: This will underline who gets what and when. (How much money does each person get from this collaboration, is it a percentage of the total amount?)
Payment time: (When do each of you get your money, monthly, quarterly, annually?)
Insurance: (Look into this if you are a collaboration using a premises to collaborate, whose funding it, is it shared between all of you?)

Painting The Picture Of Business

Emz Top Tip: - *Look into contract formats online or speak to a law form for specific advice if needed, many firms give a first session for free.*

Employing staff: - If your business needs staff, aside from insurance, you want to have people around you that share your passion and ideas to help your business grow. You need people who have vision, drive and can think outside the box. When looking for employees, you may choose to advertise online using job websites where you can list the job description and give people the chance to apply for the role and then interview them as you would any other job, whether you need receptionists for your shop or backing dancers for your performing arts company, this can be a good way of looking for the right people.

Emz Top Tip: - *When you're at a networking event meeting other business people, take note of the people you meet and whether they are looking for a job opportunity, as well as looking at what qualities you need your staff to have.*

Emma Morrissey

25/8

I have so much to do, how do I make time for all of this, when will I sleep? These are all questions you will most probably ask yourself if you start your own business as a sole trader, as there is indeed, a lot of work to do. I myself have worked myself too hard at times and have had to take a day off just to get some rest to refuel, so it is incredibly important to remember that you are not invincible and that your health is paramount.

  When I started my business, it was a real struggle to make sales and get the word out there, but it worth sticking with, as things can pick up if you keep on top of your marketing and trends in your area. It can be very difficult to make time to do everything, after all, you work for yourself and may not be in the position to delegate certain tasks to an assistant. Although I thought I was doing well under the circumstances, I slowly started to be working well into the early hours each day and often working seven days a week! Although I got work done, there wasn't the all-important structure I needed, which would give me some 'Me' time, ensure I had enough sleep and have regular breaks, after all, you get breaks for tea and lunch at work don't you, so why should your own business be any different?

By looking ahead at the next few months in my business, I was able to organize my business areas into priority sections, so that I had set times to focus on one part of my business and have the chance to put breaks into my timetable which was a real help, as a creative person I tend to continue until I have finished a project, sometimes meaning I didn't have a break for several hours which isn't healthy

Painting The Picture Of Business

I can't mention enough, the importance of keeping a diary and journal for your business; keeping a journey to record all your business activity from what day you make a sale or an order, to days of meetings and being able to make reminders to yourself on important deadlines such as emails and updates of your website and insurance renewals, this can assist with avoiding unnecessary headaches. Journals come in many different sizes which can be ideal whether you carry a briefcase or need something smaller and lighter for a handbag.

Keeping a diary, for yourself at the end of each day is a good way of recording how you are doing and coping with business life, it can be a good idea to make notes on your mood, opinions and any worries, to see when you need time to take a back seat from business and take a break before things get too overwhelming, this is a great way to avoid illness. You can get journals and diaries in all shapes and sizes from all good stationers.

Relaxation tips and techniques:

Whether it be at work, studying or juggling housework, stress affects us all in one way or another. In some cases stress can take hold and we can experience its full effects, from emotional stress which at increased levels of pressure, can lead to physical problems from general fatigue and loss of appetite to extreme exhaustion, so it is vital that you try to eliminate as many stressful situations that you can, to make things easier on yourself, this could be something very simple, like going for a walk everyday and making sure you make time in your day to have regular tea breaks and a change of scenery.

Another stress eliminating thing you could do is to make sure that your work area an area of your house that isn't your bedroom where you are more likely to spend more time.

You may have heard of the term 'Mindfulness' a lot recently, this is a technique used in CBT (Cognitive Behavioral Therapy), Counselling and Psychology, a difficult technique to master, but a helpful one. Mindfulness involved being fully aware of your situation and be aware of what is going on around you, remember to stay in the moment and can involve some meditation; this can be helpful sometimes as we can tend to go off on tangents sometimes which distracts us from the task in hand. You can find tips and books on Mindfulness in all good bookshops.

Yoga: Yoga involves exercises which can both relax and strengthen mind and body.

Meditation: Meditation can include quite spells where you 'switch off' and focus on something specific, this can be useful for relaxing or distracting yourself from a certain stressful event.

Calm place: Having a calm place in your home or work premises can be very beneficial, this could be a room with a beautiful skyline or view that has nothing to do with business to help you relax.

Deadlines: What is a deadline? Well a deadline is a task or project that has a specific due date for completion, for example, you'll find deadlines for things such as tax, insurance renewals, where there will be a certain end date and or time for its renewal. Some people work well under pressure

Painting The Picture Of Business

and sometimes it can be a good way of strengthening your skills but it can be a burden and can cause a lot of health problems such as migraine, fatigue and in some case exhaustion. So it is imperative to set out guidelines or a timetable to help you organize your time the best way to avoid health setbacks.

Many people find these very stressful and sometimes unrealistic if you have a lot of work to do and find it difficult to juggle several at once. The perfect example for this is when you have more than one deadline that overlap, this can be a real headache; for example you could have a renewal, a meeting and a presentation all due the same week, this can cause dreadful amount of stress and leave you feeling that you have no time for anything else. However, if you can prioritize these tasks and break them down into hourly tasks, you may find it will get all of the work done in a much healthier, easier to manage pace. Sometimes working backwards can be helpful.

For example:

You have three tasks all due by this coming Friday, it's currently Sunday. So all tasks need to be completed and sent out on Friday. Think to yourself, which one of these tasks is most important? Which one will take me the longest to do? With research and preparation for example and then work them into smaller chunks.

- **Presentation** will take you <u>x3 hours</u> to compile = x1 hour and 30 mins over x2 days.
- **Renewal** will take you <u>x2 hours</u> to do and it's **<u>vital</u>**. X2 hours for one day

Emma Morrissey

- **Project** will take you <u>x6 hours</u> to produce = x3 hours a day over x2 days.

So you may have a timetable that looks like this:

Monday: = x2 hours doing Renewal and x1 hour and 30mins doing Presentation
Tuesday: = x3 hours doing Project
Wednesday: = x3 hours doing Project
Thursday: = x1 hour and 30 mins finishing Presentation
Friday: = Send all completed tasks

This way you have a plan of action and a guideline to make it easier to achieve, it is important to take breaks from things so that we allow ourselves time out, so this also allows you to focus on anything else during the day that needs to be done like going food shopping.

Relaxation is crucial in business, as you are the boss after all, and therefore you may have certain responsibilities that others workers don't have to think about, such as tax, paying other business company bills, insurance, paying your employees (if you have them in your business), so you must set yourself time to yourself, this could be certain holiday breaks or long weekends away (if you have employees this may be possible to leave some responsibilities to your assistant manager whilst you are away) or if your business relies a lot of social media, you could keep an eye on business via your laptop if you really need to.

Painting The Picture Of Business

Emz Top Tip: - *It can be helpful to have a 'mobile' calm kit in your bag or briefcase, this is include a book you like to read, a bottle of essential oil or a photograph of somewhere or someone that makes you feel good and less stressed.*

Timetable – Setting yourself up a timetable can be an effective way to manage your time productively, although this will often chop and change it is good to have a guideline set out to follow, or you will be in danger of burning out through over-working.

Market Research Timetable – This highlights your main areas you wish to target your business, for example by having a list of Very Important, Important, To do and other, you can put the most imminent 'NOW' marketing jobs at the top of your list, this can help you to get through the work load.

SWOT Analysis –

A SWOT Analysis is used by each business, large or small to determine what their strengths and weaknesses are, by doing this they can see where their business strives most and what they can improve on.
S- Strengths i.e. – *Low startup costs, interest in my industry*
W- Weaknesses i.e. – *Need a car to travel to customers and for business opportunities*
O- Opportunities i.e. – *New shopping complex will bring more potential customers here*
T- Threats i.e. – *I have four competitors in my area*

Emma Morrissey

Do you have a presence?

Over the past ten years we have all been effected by it, with
one in three of us having a social media account across the
world, it is now the way most of us communicate. We all
remember the birth of Myspace, the platform which gave
musicians the opportunity to showcase and share their own
music as well as listening to their favorite bands on their own
profile pages.

Then Facebook took over, with the chance for businesses to
have a page to advertise their services makes it a very good
option as most social media platforms are free to use, but for a
small fee, you can also set up adverts on Twitter which can be
useful when you're wanting to reach certain markets with
your products or services, next time you're on Facebook you
will notice every so often a advert will pop up on the right
hand side.
With many of us aspiring to be like our favorite film and
music stars, along came Twitter, a favorite platform used by
many celebrities, it allows them to update their fans on latest
films and more and allows fans to follow their idols. Twitter is
also a great place for specialist updates about your business,
as we all get in the pattern of getting over the top with our
explanations of our businesses, however with customers often
only giving a few seconds of their concentration to one item,
this can be a big mistake, Twitter gives you the chance to only
tweet with the most crucial information due to its limited
character count, encouraging you to only include the most
important information without the fuss which could bore the
reader.

Painting The Picture Of Business

LinkedIn, what's it about? LinkedIn has been described by many as the Facebook for businesses, due to its professional appearance and C.V likeness profile which you can add your business, work and education history. You can also endorse your contacts by stating certain skills they are good at, such as Art, Illustration, meetings and more.

Blogs such as Tumblr and WordPress are popular for many now able to post their ideas, thoughts and comments and share others posts. YouTube is also a very popular platform, we also know that many singers have been discovered on YouTube by producers and music labels, so it must work? YouTube can be a good way of showcasing your products with a short promotional film and linking it to your website or doing a live stream.

Emz Top Tip: - *When making a short film, if you have several clips that you want to put together, a good tool is Windows Movie Maker, which allows you to put several clips together, with titles, text, music and transitions, making a good quality promotional film for your business and is fairly easy to use compared to other programs.*

Having a Social Media presence is becoming more and more important in business as you will find a lot of local businesses, whether it be coffee shops, shopping centers and more will have a Facebook page or a Twitter account in order to reach a wider range of people, if you already have a personal profile for yourself, it may be worth you looking at which one gets the most activity, how many people check your page per day? How many new people browse your page? This might give you a good insight into which platforms will give you the most activity for your business.

Emma Morrissey

<u>Competitions:</u> Competitions are still very popular, from cereal packets to the chance to win cars and holidays, there are many out there to suit each person and are often very simple and affordable to enter, they help raise awareness for the company involved giving away the offer in the hope that people will think to use the business in the future.

Having a competition on your social media profile can be a great way of encouraging activity, this may be an event which links to your website, where the person could be with the chance to win a product by completing a short survey or giving suggestions.

<u>Social Media Timetable</u> – Making a calendar for your Social Media updates will help you to organize what platform you use for your business and when, this will help you save time in your week by setting aside specific time for each one and avoid wasting time you could be spending on more important business matters.

<u>Facebook</u>: May be good to set up a business page and for creating events on your business page.

<u>Twitter:</u> May be good for creating hashtags for current trends. LinkedIn: May be useful to create a profile in order to network with other businesses.

<u>Blogger:</u> May be a great idea for you to create a blog for your business which you can update with regular events, sales and more. You can find templates for all these at the back of the book.

Painting The Picture Of Business

Month	Current	Wk 1	Wk 2	Month Notes	Wk 5	Wk 6	Wk 7	Wk 8
W/e beg		23/03/2015	30/03/2015		06/04/2015	13/04/2015	20/04/2015	27/04/2015
Blog								
articles	1				0	1		
visits			1		2	4		
guest blogs	0		0		0	0		
visits			1		8	4		
follows	1		3		3	4		
Twitter								
followers	29		31		31	38	36	38
following	101	102	103		116	116	116	132
mentions	0		0		0	0	0	0
retweets	2	3	0		7	5	1	0
hashtags	2	3	0		0	0	5	
leads								
Facebook								
follows								
likes	47	48	48		48	49	52	54
engagements		2			29	33	4	6
referring traffic					29	33	66	74

Example of a Social Media calendar to keep track of activity on each platform, which can be created in Excel.

Bits and Blogs:

The best place to start when considering starting your own business, is a Business Plan, this is a document where you details all aspects of your business, what will it be? How much money do you need to run it? How many competitors do you have? How will you cope if you have a dry month with no business? All these ideas are worth asking, to give you an idea if your business would be plausible and earn you money. See the templates section for tips on this.

Starting a blog can be a tricky thing as many blog platforms offer many designs and templates which gives you the choice to spend hours creating the perfect blog, this is worth doing, as blogging is becoming more and more popular, from fashion journalists to opinion polls, people are blogging as a way to tell the world their thoughts, feelings and even a place to share creative writing and lyrics, so you can really use it for pretty much anything.

Emma Morrissey

Blog content is interesting, I find that keeping an eye on news and by flicking through magazines can be a good way of collecting content that is relevant to your business and therefore can be a good way of starting to write in your own blog. Look at some blogs online and pay attention to the layout, the content and how much interest is gets, some blogs offer links to other writing sites which can give you an insight on how to go about writing a blog, they also offer competitions as well, which can be a good way to test your skill and get some important feedback from people, this is all good practice.

Your first blog post: keep in mind the content, read it back to yourself, is it too long, it is catchy, and do you want to read on? How is the layout, is it visual, does it need images (remember it is best to use your own images if you can, as many images found on online search engines you may need permission to use), remember to link it back to your website!

Newsletters: What is a newsletter I hear you ask, well, you'll find when you go onto some of your favorite websites, you may be asked to sign up to their monthly newsletter, this is basically a collaboration of that businesses latest news, upcoming events and special offers all in one letter. Why are these a good idea? Well, many businesses can keep track of how many people are signing up for their newsletters, therefore giving them direct feedback on how much activity and potential sales their business may get from this, it also allows the business the opportunity to offer its customers special offers such as buy one get one free or 10% off, to encourage customers to buy now rather than later.

Painting The Picture Of Business

Emz Portraits & Crafts.
'Where your special moments are Works of Art.'

May Newsletter 2015.

Art Exhibition on the water!

My Fine Art Exhibition is coming! From May 26th at Harbour Lights Picture House Cinema in Ocean Village in Southampton with free admission.

Venue: Harbour Lights Picture House Cinema
Dates: 26th May - June 23rd 2015
Time: Weekdays 11am-11pm.

Please see the links below for details

Discover Southampton!
See my Exhibition on the Discover Southampton website Events page.

Upcoming Events:

Art Workshops coming in September!

Contact Details:

Email: emzportraitscrafts@gmail.com
Facebook: /emzportraitscrafts
Twitter: @emzportraits

Example of one of my Newsletters.

'Personal Survival Budget' or PSB - this is a run-down of all your expenses per month, by limiting yourself to your essentials you can see the basic amount of money you need to earn, this is particularly helpful in the early days of a business as all small businesses start up slowly and may not see a profit until their second or third year as the first year in business is spent on startup materials costs and getting the word out there to establish customers. Common things to list in your PSB would be, bills, Broadband, food and drink, medication, Phone bill, car and home insurance/mortgage etc.

Emma Morrissey

<u>Unique Selling Point or USP</u> - this in basic terms means, in an industry of several businesses offering a similar product or service, what makes your business better and different from all the rest? Do you offer introductory prices, discount on next purchases, do you have specialist experience that others don't etc.

Emz Top Tip – *Your USP (Unique Selling Point) is worth spending some time on, to drill down exactly what you can offer as a business that others can't. For example, do you have a unique quality or product that puts you above your competitors? Can to travel to several places for business opportunity? Do you have another job which will help with business costs? Are you good with paperwork and making lists?*

<u>Social Media</u> - as social media is used by billions across the world, it makes sense to take advantage of the free platforms that are currently available, such as Facebook pages, Twitter ads, Blogs and LinkedIn - a brilliant networking site set up for businesses to network with each-other.

<u>Market Research/Marketing Strategy</u> – Market Research is a must for any business, it can help you find where you fit in your market industry and help you determine where your customers are. The more research you do the clearer it will become what strategy you choose to use, it may be that you choose to do most of not all of your business online if the market is strong enough there, or you may decide to conduct your business in a premises if your customers are keen shoppers are therefore would benefit from walking into your shop.

Painting The Picture Of Business

Emz Top Tip – *Create Market Research Surveys on Word to print out and give to people to answer a few simple questions like, how much would you expect to pay for this product/service? What is important to you as a customer? What would encourage you to buy again?*

Promotion/Advertising – after you've done your market research a lot of your promotional opportunities may become clearer, social media is the best place to start as a lot of it is free to use and therefore is a great way to raise awareness of your business and what you do.

One of my business fliers.

Emz Top Tip. - *You can create your own flyers via software online.. This can save you a lot of time and money if you decide to design your own.*

It is also worth noting that the old saying 'If you don't ask, you don't get' is still relevant in most cases including business. I often consider my target markets and how I could reach more customers, sending tailored emails to shops may by an option, the more people you connect with the better chance you have of getting your name seen by someone.

Emma Morrissey

Sales Recorder:

A Sales Recorder is a spreadsheet which labels each month of the year and have the products/Services you offer in columns, you can enter how many of that product/service you sold each month and how much each unit cost. This is a great way to record your Monthly sales, this will also help you to physically see which areas of your business are selling well and which ones aren't.

Emz Top Tip: - *You can create a Sales Recorder spreadsheet in Excel. You can search for templates online.*

Painting The Picture Of Business

The legal Stuff:

The legal side of business is essential otherwise, you don't have a business. However, this is also often the reason people don't take that final step, as the legal side including tax, insurance and more, can be a real headache, so it is important to find out as much information that applies specifically to your business as possible before you even think about starting a business.

HMRC - When you start a business and have started trading, you must register as a Self Employed person on the HMRC website, if you don't register you could face penalty charges or even prosecution, as soon as you have registered your business this will allow you to do your tax return each year and register for the online Self-Assessment tax return which you can do online. It will also allow you to pay your National Insurance contributions. Its true tax is taxing but if you know the basics it can help make things a bit easier, depending what tax year you start your business, you will have to fill out a Self-Assessment tax return for that tax year, stating what your business has earned through stating your Gross and Net Profit.

The personal allowance for tax at 2017/18 is currently £11.500 with 20% tax payment on anything earnt over that amount, (**Please check the HMRC website for details on this as current estimations in this book may have been changed**)

Emma Morrissey

Emz Top Tip: - *If you are new to filling out tax returns, it might be worth getting in contact with a registered accountant, who can give you advice and quotes for doing your tax return for you, this can save you time and money, as well as avoiding a headache, however if your business isn't likely to earn more than the personal allowance then you may be advised to do the tax return yourself if you can.*

As of April 2016, the way that National Insurance Contributions were collected will change and shall be collected through your tax return.

National Insurance - these are the payments you are issued by HMRC depending on what type of business you are, Class 2 or Class4, as a Sole Trader, Limited Company etc. These payments contribute to possible maternity pay, bereavement and pensions.

Business Expenses - It is important to keep all receipts you spend on your business, so if you're an Artist doing commissions for example, any Art materials you buy to create Artwork for your customers, phone top-ups, in order to speak to your customers, fuel costs to business meetings etc. It is important to remember that anything you state as a business expense must be spent on your business and not for personal use.

Business Account: - It is important to open a separate bank account for your business income, this makes your bookkeeping easier.

Painting The Picture Of Business

Emz Top Tip – *Ensure you keep all receipts of purchases you make for your business, from materials you need, to phone credit to speak to your customers, make sure the receipts you have are for your business and not for personal use. This will help you keep track of things and make your tax return easier, the best way to record this in by filling in a cash-flow spreadsheet, if you have Microsoft Office, then you can do this in Excel. There are also many templates in Excel which you can use, here is a basic blank one which you can create.*

Cash sales						
Other employment						
Bacs & card payments						
Taxable benefits						
Wages						
Materials						
Advertising -website costs						
Rent						
Electric						
Gas						
Water						
Mobile phone						
Landline/broadband package						
Insurance						
VAT						
Nat Insurance						
Car fuel						
Public transport costs						
other						

Public Liability Insurance – this is important for creatives who work in a public place i.e. a photographer doing a photo shoot at a public event, or an Artisan having a craft stall at a local craft fayre, public Liability insurance insures you against any accidents to you or anyone else, for example, if someone tripped on your craft stall table. You can check for quotes on public liability insurance with several companies offering insurance.

Emma Morrissey

Other types of Insurance:
If your business revolves around it, insure it. A lot of artisans from illustrators, photographers to sculptors as their business relies on the artistic use of their hands in order to create their products and in some cases for a person freelance or with a company in the Performing Arts, a dancer might think to insure their legs in case of an accident and needing to take time off to recover or a vocalist insuring their vocal chords as many famous singers experience various problems from chest infections to internal bleeds which can be fatal to a singer. You can get more information online by researching insurance companies or get some independent advice from a law or insurance firm.

Employee Insurance:
If your business requires several people and you need to employ people, you will need to insure them all for accidents purposes for example. You will also need insurance if your business does work overseas, this may be into insure a van which crosses the ocean or stock that travels abroad to a customer for example. You can get quotes for this on insurance websites.

DBS Check - if you are a creative person who may work with children or vulnerable people, all establishments will ask for you to have a DBS check, to check that you have a clear police record and are therefore legal to work with children and vulnerable people.

Emz Top Tip – *If you work already in another job, you may have had a DBS check already as some employers do checks when recruiting new staff, check with your employer.*

Painting The Picture Of Business

Copyright:

If you are a designer or artist or some description and you create pieces for your customers than you hold the copyright for those pieces of work, however, if you are graphic designer doing work for a company designing their logo for example, you will need to research how this will work best for you as many designers will sell the logo design to the company, including the copyright so best to look into this so you know what you want to own in terms of copyright.

Emz Top Tip: - *When placing any work online for others to look at or save for their own personal use, watermark it with your name or business name on it and year of creation, this will ensure that people know it belongs to you. For any more details on this, you can find lots of useful information on copyright and watermarks online or through a law firm.*

NDA:-You may have come across this when reading about inventions, an NDA is a Non-Disclosure Agreement, many inventors use this to ensure that a new idea, design or invention is not shared with anyone else, to ensure that it is not stolen and created by someone else or seen by a competitor.

Patent: -You may have seen these used for beauty products or new ideas from companies. A patent is an agreement between a company, or inventor for the rights to use it, for an agreed time slot which will state some details of the product or invention which may have offered a solution to a problem.

Health and Safety – The Health and Safety Act 1974, applies to all businesses which have a premises, employers and employees, this is to ensure that the premises and the people

81

Emma Morrissey

working there are insured and advised on the health and safety act, this is important so that your customers know that the products/services you offer are created/produced in a safe, clean environment.

This can involve many things such as fire assembly, food safety and in some cases high visibility jackets, food hygiene will apply if you run a café for example, as all kitchen utensils and cooking equipment and consumable goods must be free of any item that can cause either a fire hazard or contamination, such as bins which carry dirt, bacteria etc.

It is very important that in business, all people are taught about Health and Safety, you may have come across this in shops or on premises, for example; you will find signs around many places detailing the fire assembly point and where to find a fire extinguisher.

You will also come across certificates up in many food venues detailing their level from 1-5 on how they met food safety and hygiene carried out by local authorities. Food hygiene includes having designated areas for food preparation for both raw and cooked foods to ensure they do not overlap and cause a contamination which could lead to food poisoning such as salmonella and E.coli; it is also important to have a designated area for the washing up and disposal of food and waste in a safe area, for example, if you run a beauty salon, you must ensure that all bins are away from kitchen areas so that materials such as hair, liquids etc. as well as any other waste does not interfere and cause any form of bacteria. In premises it is important that all workers and visitors are aware of fire drills and where to find a first aid kit, you may have noticed these in various places.

Painting The Picture Of Business

Another important thing you may have come across is to
ensure there are no trip hazards in public places such as shops,
for example, when cleaning a floor in a shop, you will notice
that a yellow sign will be put out, so that all customers are
aware of the slippery floor, this also applies to fire doors,
which must be kept clear, for example, if a delivery has been
made and an item has been left to block the fire door, then in
case of a fire, people may not be able to get out which could
be fatal so the importance of health and safety is a must to
ensure that all products are created in a safe and clean
environment and that all premises are equipped with fire
extinguishers and safety signs.

Emz Top Tip: - *If you are starting a business, it is vital that you
find out what health and safety will apply to you and your business
and employees.*

When thinking about starting your own business, it is essential
that you get your own independent legal advice, many legal
firms will give you the first hour free of charge, for any
financial advice, it is best to get an appointment with your
local bank, as they have advisors that can give you advice on
business startup loans and more.

Emma Morrissey

Templates: Here are some basic templates for you to use:

Emz Top Tip:
Do you have Windows 8 or more and Microsoft Office newer editions? Word offers some great templates for many things from a business cards to a business plan.

Here are some templates for you to use:
- Business Plan
- PSB - Add this to your Business plan
- USP - Add this to your Business Plan
- SWOT Analysis
- Cash flow forecast
- Timetable
- Market Research Survey
- Marketing Plan/Strategy
- Social Media Timetable
- Business cards
- Sales Recorder

Business Plan Run-thru (fictitious example below):

Business Name: *Potters Pottery*
Business Roles: *Managing Director/Assistant/Accountant etc.*
How will I run the business? *Home run/office*
Business Goals for first year: *Locating customers/advertising in directory/flyer dropping*
Financial Forecast: *How much money do I need to earn to get by?*
Marketing: *Business cards/flyers/radio advert/shop*
Target Market: *Pet owners/families/other businesses*
Do I need funding/sponsorship? *Council/grants from government*

Painting The Picture Of Business

<u>Draft your Business Plan here</u>
<u>Notes:</u>

Emma Morrissey

<u>Personal Survival Budget: On a monthly basis</u>
<u>You can find good templates online.</u>

Food shop =
Landline Phone bill =
Mobile Phone bill =
Mortgage/rent =
Home Insurance/Contents insurance =
Water bill =
Electric bill =
Gas bill =
Car Insurance =
Children costs, clothes, school materials etc. =
Other =

Painting The Picture Of Business

<u>USP - Unique Selling Point</u>

What makes my Business different?
What will make my business marketable in my industry?
How I intend to attract my customers?
Where are my customers?
How am I going to get to my customers?

<u>Work on your USP (Unique Selling Point) here</u>
<u>Notes:</u>

Emma Morrissey

SWOT Analysis
A SWOT analysis is a detailed timetable of four main areas of your business, this will help you to discover what parts of your business need work:

Draft your own SWOT Analysis here:

Strength	Weaknesses
Opportunity	**Threats**

Painting The Picture Of Business

Cash Flow Forecast
You can find some good templates online as well as creating one in Excel, most of these will add up the figures for you, it is a very important tool to have when it comes to doing your tax return! This may breakdown, to look something like this.

Cash sales
Part time or full time job
Any other income

Business Expenses:
Mobile phone, materials, insurance, national insurance, car etc.

Gross Income
Net income
Income less expenditure.

Emma Morrissey

Here is an example of some of these put into an Excel spreadsheet, you can find templates in Excel as well if you have the latest version of Microsoft Office.

Cash sales								
Other employment								
Bacs & card payments								
Taxable benefits								
Wages								
Materials								
Advertising -website costs								
Rent								
Electric								
Gas								
Water								
Mobile phone								
Landline/broadband package								
Insurance								
VAT								
Nat Insurance								
Car fuel								
Public transport costs								
other								

Painting The Picture Of Business

<u>Timetable:</u>
Once you have arranged the hours you work in a week, you can set out a timetable to help, something like this:

- 9am – 10am =
- 10am – 10.30am = break
- 10.30am – 12pm =
- 12pm – 12.30pm = Lunch
- 12.30pm - 2pm =
- 2pm – 3pm =
- 3pm – 3.30pm = break
- 3.30pm – 5pm =

Emma Morrissey

Market Research Survey

Market Research Surveys are a great way to get feedback on your proposed business from many different people, these are a good way to get insight before you set up your business and they are also very good to do throughout your business once you have started, by creating tailored questions on different areas of your business to find out how your business is doing.

How often would you use my business services or buy my products?

Once a month   several times a month

Special Occasions   Annually

How much would you consider paying for these services/products?

Marketing Plan/Strategy

My Business would benefit from marketing in local/broad area

I will conduct online marketing research

My Target Markets are –

Target 1

Target 2

Target 3

Painting The Picture Of Business

The way to get each of these target markets are:
1
2
3

Work on your Marketing Plan here
Notes:

Emma Morrissey

<u>Social Media Timetable</u>
When you conduct your Social Media Timetable, you need to conduct your own research into which Social Media platforms will benefit you the most.

Emz Top Tip - *On Facebook you can set up a page for your business for free, once your page has 30 likes you can look at the 'Insights' tab which will show you how many people are seeing your updates etc.*

You can set up a Twitter account for a business and both Facebook and Twitter offer Adverts, which you can set a payment limit to.
LinkedIn is a great way to network with other business owners so is good for B2B (Business to Business) i.e. your customer is a business not an everyday consumer.

Monday – Tumblr/Facebook/Pinterest
Tuesday
Wednesday – Wordpress/Twitter
Thursday
Friday – LinkedIn

Painting The Picture Of Business

Create your Social Media Timetable here
Notes:

Emma Morrissey

<u>Business Cards:</u>
A Business card is the port of call for all businesses, it allows you to give vital information to your contacts at networking meetings and to potential customers. Here's an example of what to include.

Business name:
Your name and business title:
Your tagline (If you have one) this will be a phrase which says what you and your business does
An image
Email:
Website:
Phone:

There are some great templates for making your own business cards online and in Word if you have Microsoft office, or there are many online shops which offer to print and make the business cards for you.

<u>Design your Business Cards here:</u>

Painting The Picture Of Business

Sales Recorder Example:

A Sales Recorder is a spreadsheet which shows your sales in the year applicable, it can help you see what money your business has earnt and show you what months are good for business and vice versa. This could look something like this (example below)

	A	B	C	D	E
1	Photography Prints A5				
2					
3	Photography Prints A4				
4					
5	Photography package				
6					
7	Photoshoot orders A4				
8					
9	Photoshoot orders A3				
10					
11					
12					
13					
14					
15					
16					

With months written in boxes along the top and your products down the side and price per item and a total box, so for example: If you sold x2 photographs which are £35.00 each. Price per item would be 35 with a total of £70.00.
You can find templates online and in Excel for Sales Recorders.

Emma Morrissey

<u>Draft what your Sales Recorder would look like here:</u>
<u>Notes:</u>

Painting The Picture Of Business

Hints and Phrases

GROSS INCOME = All of your business income, including your expenses.
NET INCOME = your business profit, after you've taken off your expenses.
Profit = If your business made more money than it spent.
Loss = If your business spent more money than it made.
B2B = Business to Business
B2C = Business to Consumer
USP = Unique Selling Point
PSB = Personal Survival Budget
AVO = Average Value Order
Pitch or Elevator Pitch = your sales pitch (to put it bluntly)
Close of Business = the end of business on the particular day
i.e. most business days are 9am – 5pm.
Let's talk shop = let's talk business.

Emma Morrissey

What Do I Do Now?

Time: Is a must in any business and it makes sense to plan as much as you can so that you have as much information about how your business will run? What is your target market? And how much money you need to make and how you intend to reach your customers?

No knowledge is ever wasted, so spend time getting to know how to run your business in the most efficient way for you, It is also worth looking into local day courses which often run in Business Centre's in cities across England, from Marketing to Book-keeping, all this will help prepare you for what it takes to run a business, it is also important to remember that all businesses work differently, a strategy that works for one company, may not work for another, some will be able to work from home, some will need an office premises, one may need a part time job to support their business or may take out a loan whereas some may have smaller expenses and therefore may hit a profit.

Emz Top Tip: - *It's worth looking into local volunteer work you could get involved in, this could be working for a business and handing out flyers, it may give you an insight into how business works and give you some ideas on what you want to do and if your business idea is feasible?*

Having your own strategy that works for your business is essential to making it work in the most effective way, taking the time to research all of this is important in the early days to avoid discovering it later, I took a year to find out as much as I could before I knew the time was right, so don't worry if you need the same or more time, the more time you take, the

Painting The Picture Of Business

stronger your business will be when you first start out, because you don't want to make big decisions like loans or re-mortgaging if there are still some financial aspects that you haven't considered.

Emz Top Tip *–Keep a copy of everything you use for your business, this includes everything from receipts of business equipment, to business emails, orders that come through and important letters! Trust me, it helps.*

It is also a good idea to get yourself a simple ring-binder folder to hold important business information in, that way you have all the relevant information together in one place, for easy access when you need it.

Contacts:-Make notes of important people who you could network with and look at events you could attend and join, all this can be good preparation until you make a decision on whether to start a business or not. Look in local business newspapers, your local libraries may have some useful information.

T.V:-I know, I'm actually telling you to watch T.V, however, some business focused programs can give you a great insight into the different areas of business; programs such as Dragons Den can be helpful. So get your notebook out when watching and make notes on business pitches, what mistakes did they make? What would you do differently?

Books:-Read as much as you can, as gaining as much information on your market before you start could put you ahead of the game.

Emma Morrissey

Finance:-A lot of businesses struggle, or fail either through low knowledge of their market and target audience, or because they run out of money. Focus on your PSB first.

PSB (Personal Survival Budget) so you have a solid idea of what you need to earn in order to afford your everyday bills and how much your business needs to make for you to be able to live comfortably so having a backup plan in sensible, this may be a part time job for example. Something that allows you to pay your bills if your business takes a while setting up.

Entrepreneurial thinking:-More and more people are thinking in a new, creative way, researching into new ways of thinking and planning can help broaden your horizons whilst realizing the potential of ideas and which ones have promise and which ones need work.

What if I can't do it? - If it doesn't work, don't worry too much, many businesses go through this, it is just one of those things. That's why lots of businesses do market research until its 'coming out of their ears' so to speak, to avoid the 'it's not working' sensation. It can also help you determine whether your business will be successful in terms of feasibility and profitability.
If you can do it, but not yet, this isn't a bad thing either, whether you don't have enough money to set up or the right experience, you may find that a break to get the knowledge you need may be the best option for you as well as the proposed business. It's very easy to jump in 'head first' through excitement but you need to be sensible, this is going to be a big part of life and livelihood after all so you want to get it right.

Painting The Picture Of Business

Useful Information:

HMRC – For details on TAX, VAT, Benefits and more.

Business Insurance – You will find many companies that offer several types of insurance for business, from Liability to Employer insurance, search for quotes on insurances such as Public Liability

Website building – Thee are many platforms that you can use to create your own website and domain names, find them in directories or online.

Blogs – You will find many different platforms which allow you to build your own blog, find them online.

Printing services – There are many websites which cater for all your marketing materials including business cards, flyers and more, there are also some printing shops that offer this service.

Photo services – For artists and photographers, there are websites and shops where you can get photo books, if you are an Artist/illustrator, model or photographer, you can use this as a way of created a great portfolio to show potential customers! Simply upload your images and order.

Libraries: You may choose to visit your local library to get some advice on local businesses and to research.

Emma Morrissey

Finance: You may find advice in your local bank or building society, as most will have a business advisor who you may be able to get some business advice from on finance, from loans to business accounts.

Business Centers: Search your local Business Centers for any day workshops and sign up to newsletters and blogs to do from valued businesses to give you as much information as possible.

Painting The Picture Of Business

Emma Morrissey

Painting the Picture of Business.

This is a help and advice book for people wanting to find out more about setting up a small business, you must ensure you have considered all aspects of your chosen business venture. You must also be certain on all payments your business may include like VAT, National Insurance, as well as Tax and Insurances before you consider starting a business.

This book is in no way held accountable for decisions made by readers to start a business and is not accountable for failed or financial crisis of those businesses.

This book is intended for the purposes of providing information and advice only and is not by any means an exact representation of how to start a business, but told from one perspective and should be seen as inspiration and advice only.

All information of websites and legal advice can be found on HMRC's website and was correct at the time of this book's publication.

Painting The Picture Of Business

Emma Morrissey

About The Author:

Emma Morrissey is a Fine Artist and business woman in the South of England, creating custom Artwork for her clients and teaching Art and Enterprise. After completing her Degree, setbacks and the slump of unemployment; through determination and training, Emma pursued her dreams and set up her business in 2014. Now a published book cover Artist, exhibiting across Hampshire and teaching and mentoring, Emma is passionate about using her experience to help others wanting to find out about small business in the creative world. *"I decided to put my knowledge and experience into this book to help you to explore the options of your dreams."* 2016

Painting The Picture Of Business

www.ingramcontent.com/pod-product-compliance
Lightning Source LLC
Chambersburg PA
CBHW071213200326
41519CB00018B/5501